Simple Self-Defense Techniques Everyone Should Know

Amazing Common Sense Techniques That Empower You With The Knowledge You Need To Win.

By Lee Shaykhet

Copyright © Lee Shaykhet and Rich LifeStyles Network

About Lee Shaykhet.

Lee Shaykhet was born in Moscow, Russia (former Soviet Union). He graduated from the University of Moscow and was involved in training for the military.

In 1979 Lee came to the US and has been involved in law enforcement and civilian training ever since.

Lee regularly conducts self-defense, edged weapons, firearms, ground applications and SWAT training.

He is also a public speaker and an expert witness.

Lee has made numerous television appearances including a recent appearance on FOX News as a training expert, following a police shooting that injured multiple Police Officers in Detroit.

Lee teaches simple, practical self-defense techniques. His training is proven to work in real life.

Police officers use his training every day to control dangerous criminals.

Lee's training is directly responsible for helping members of law enforcement and

Civilians defend themselves and avoid injury.

Lee has taught at The International Law Enforcement Educators and Trainers

Association (ILEETA) for the past 3 years.

He is also an instructor for TEAM ONE NETWORK, a law enforcement training

Organization.

Table of Contents.

1. Introduction	**7**
2. Self Defense for Law Enforcement	**10**
3. Self Defense for Women and Men	**14**
4. Self Defense for Children	**30**
5. Self Defense Differences	**34**
6. Firearms Applications	**40**
7. Firearms Training	**50**
8. Ground Applications	**61**
9. Edged Weapons	**64**
10. The Importance of Vision	**69**

11. Situational Awareness   **71**

12. Conclusion   **73**

Introduction.

Since the beginning of life there has always been the need for self-defense.

There will always be dangerous people willing to hurt and even kill others.

These individuals have no regard for human life and therefore pose a threat that must be stopped.

My mission is to help people by teaching them how to protect themselves and avoid getting hurt or killed.

It just takes some basic understanding and willingness to learn. It is not difficult.

The goal of this book is to empower people and arm them with the knowledge needed so they will be able to defend and protect themselves.

Self-defense is a basic life skill that is essential for survival. Regardless of where you live, you have some level of exposure to danger.

Some have more exposure, some have less based on their location and the activities they engage in.

The ability to defend one's self dramatically improves the quality of everyday life by giving people confidence.

Law enforcement officers, men, women, children, the elderly and even people with physical challenges can defend themselves effectively.

There are some simple, basic, natural ideas that explain self-defense applications.

These concepts are user friendly for everyone. This book represents an optimized

version of self-defense that is easy to understand and apply.

Self-defense at its core is pretty basic.

There are numerous examples of people getting hurt or even killed by a deranged person.

Tragic incidents like Columbine, Virginia Tech, and most recently Sandy Hook Elementary School come to mind. Large numbers of people were killed and wounded.

Often times, there is a gun or a knife involved. Some people think that if the bad guy has a gun that automatically means that now all is lost and there is nothing they can do to defend themselves.

That is false.

A lot of deaths and injuries can be prevented by simply understanding what to do under these extreme conditions.

The positive message contained here is that self-defense applications can be easily learned and applied in critical circumstances with dramatic results.

It works even when the bad guy has a weapon.

Again, this is all about knowledge and understanding what to do.

You definitely have the ability to defend yourself. All you have to do is learn the basics.

Knowledge makes you feel confident every day.

The message of this book is simple: **you are not a victim, you will have a positive mental attitude, you will be prepared, you will win the confrontation, you will survive.**

Self Defense for Law Enforcement.

I have been teaching Law Enforcement since I first came to America in 1979.

Over the years thousands of officers have went through my training. They use my training every day in real life situations. It is extremely rewarding to hear from them when they use my techniques and it prevents problems. I've had numerous examples of my training actually saving someone's life or preventing them from getting hurt.

This is the reason I do what I do.

Unfortunately, a lot of traditional police training follows step by step procedures that do not work at all in real life. It is almost as if no one cares if the officer or the subject gets hurt.

As an example, at the end of every class I teach, I

end with a debriefing. I ask every officer there to say a few words as a comment on my class, things that stand out and examples that come to mind.

I hear the same responses over and over, regardless of where I teach.

An veteran officer will stand up and share comments such as "I've been in Law Enforcement for 20 years. I have been hurt several times fighting with people. I sure wish I knew then what you showed us today. I would not have gotten hurt then."

A brand new officer will get up and say "I just graduated from the police academy. They put me through 40 hours of defensive tactics" (police speak for self-defense).

"If you ask me now to do it, I can't. It's too complicated. Your program only took three hours and I can apply what I learned right away. It is simple. Why didn't they teach me this at the academy?"

I hear these types of comments all the time and have an answer.

It seems people in the positions of power over training, like at the police academy, often prefer to leave things alone. They don't want to rock the boat.

As one of my students, a police officer in the Chicago area correctly pointed out, **"The only person who likes a change is a wet baby."** That is a true statement.

Of course there are some people in training who are progressive. They don't want to see their people hurt. These people love my training, but sadly they are often in the
minority.

In police work it is important to have a simple, effective way of dealing with combative subjects (bad guys).

My training is really simple. No fancy steps. You don't have to go home and do a million repetitions.

Police officers have a very difficult job. On the one hand they must be able to control the subject.

On the other hand, unless it is a life threatening situation, they don't want to be
perceived as hurting people.

There are always stories and videos about police brutality. It is a difficult balance that they have to achieve. My training gives them capability to control subjects right away. This prevents people from getting hurt. It also looks humane. No police brutality here.

I believe when we ask police officers to go out there and handle dangerous situations, the least we can do is to give them relevant training to minimize their chances of getting hurt.

By relevant I mean something that actually works in real life. That is my take.

Some of the training that I do deals with handcuffing,

searching, ground applications, edged weapons, firearms, SWAT training, etc., in other words anything that involves practical applications in the field.

I happily speak to any Law Enforcement entity interested in my training.

Self Defense for Women and Men

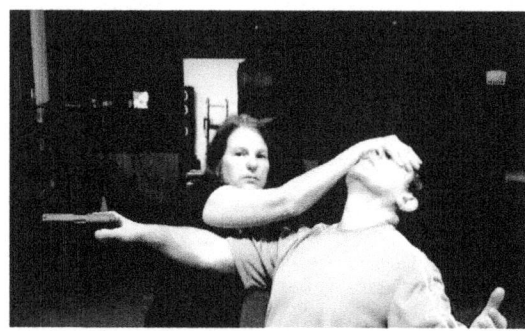

Traditionally, there is a view that it's almost impossible for women to defend themselves especially against a big bad guy, since they usually are physically smaller and have less upper body strength. In other words, in a confrontation it's all about muscle. Bigger muscles win the fight. Nothing can be further from the truth.

Yes, muscle plays a role but real effective self-defense has very little to do with size or muscle.

It is all about tactics.

First of all, a human being is a predator. Yes, a predator.

That is not my opinion. It is a scientific fact. There have been various studies done to analyze skulls of various animals. These studies determine that you can differentiate the skull of a predator from that of a prey animal based on location of the eyes on the skull.

If the eyes are in the front, that is a predator. Two eyes focused on the target (prey animal) with overlapping fields of view provide a crystal clear image, which is necessary for the successful hunt. It comes at the expense of peripheral vision, which is somewhat limited.

The example of predators are lions, tigers, humans, bears, wolves, cats, dogs, birds of prey, etc.

Prey animals, on the other hand, have their eyes located on the side of the head to give them a wide field of view. That way they can see danger approaching even if they are not looking directly at it. The example of prey animals are horses, deer, rabbits, turkeys, antelope, etc.

Here is an easy way to remember the difference between predator and prey: **Eyes in front - born to hunt, eyes on the side - born to hide.**

Therefore, since a human is a predator, I believe that during a confrontation he **or** she should act like one.

To make this point, let's examine how the predator acts.

For example, if we look at a pride of lions in Africa, we can see the predatory technique in action.

Interestingly, even though the male lions are much larger than females, it is the female lioness that does the majority of the hunting.

These lionesses routinely take down animals that are

far bigger, heavier and have a lot more muscle.

If you look at the size of the zebra, to pick an example, it is much larger that a lioness.

Clearly, it is not a matter of muscle or weight. It is the tactics that matter.

The Lioness approaches the zebra from behind, so that zebra cannot see it. When the lioness is close enough, she makes a fast dash to close the distance to the target, then grabs the zebra by the head or neck, puts it down on the ground, and you might say: **dinner is served.**

This process from start to finish does not take long. It is over within a few seconds. **I call it: quick closure**.

In my training that concept of quick closure is applied to real life confrontations.

Just like a lioness, a woman can defend herself, her children and family. She just needs to understand the predatory tactics. That way the big guy that is trying to assault her is just a big zebra, so to speak and can be taken down and controlled in the same fashion by executing a head grab take down.

These concepts are sometimes difficult to relate to at first because they seem foreign from what people are used to. They represent an entirely different way of thinking.

Some of the misconceptions result from watching movies and television.

The common portrayal of confrontations on TV has nothing to do with reality. It should come with a disclaimer, such as: **this program is just entertainment. Do not take it seriously.**

For one thing these scenes are usually protracted and take a long time.

In reality everything typically ends very quickly. It is not a long story.

Another point is that people equate self-defense with martial arts.

That is not the same thing at all and is a common misconception.

Martial arts by nature are more complex and take a much longer time to master.

Martial Arts are very good for discipline and sports. But not always the case in matters of self-defense.

Human beings are simply not capable of doing complicated step by step procedures under stress, and the bad guy is not going to stand still for half an hour waiting for all steps to be perfectly done.

By the way, if even one step is not done right, the whole thing can fall apart.

I would call that approach: **wishful thinking.**

Practical defensive applications are different from

martial arts like day and night. Then there is the issue of what we in the U.S. call **fairness.**

People get an idea from watching movies, that we have to fight **fair and square**.

This makes no sense whatsoever.

If we were to apply that logic to the lioness, she would have to approach the zebra head on. Just to be fair. That clearly is a flawed strategy because the zebra then would be able to see the lioness and just run away.

The lioness trying that approach did not survive. They died off. The ones who survived, learned fairness, when it comes to getting the prey does not work.

Likewise, when a woman is being assaulted, we are way passed the fairness doctrine. Now it is about winning the fight.

When I first came to the United States, I heard that it doesn't matter who wins or loses, rather how we play the game, or something like that. In some instances it is true. However, when it comes to self defense, I disagree with that. That thinking will get you hurt or even killed.

When it comes to physical assaults, it matters very much who wins and who loses. Failure is definitely not an option here. **We are here to win.**

My rule of engagement is simple: We will win and

the bad guy will lose.

And I would call that fair. I want to point out that I do not have twenty different rules.

That is the only rule I have. A bit like a lioness.

Let's further analyze exactly how does the lioness goes about taking down the zebra in more detail.

Once the initial contact is made, the lioness stays locked in on the zebra. There is no daylight (distance) between the lioness and the zebra.

She grabs the zebra's head and uses her body weight to put it down on the ground.

That is what we have to do as well.

Basically, we will grab the bad guy by the head and put him on the ground.

It's all over. It's that simple.

Then the whole pride of lions shows up and feeds.

For the record, I want to point out that we are not going to eat the bad guy (just kidding). Other than that, the concepts are exactly the same.

Since I do a lot of training for Law Enforcement, we actually use these concepts in real life applications every day and it works great. The bad guy stands no chance. He has no idea of what is happening.

A lot of women now work in Law Enforcement. They use my training all the time.

The typical comment I get from women is how much they enjoy my training and how well it works for them in the field, as opposed to the traditional step by step procedures that not only do not work, but get people hurt.

Again, the basic concept is **quick closure.** We do not want a prolonged exposure to the bad guy.

Generally, the longer it takes to get the situation under control, the greater the possibility of getting hurt.

Also, if the confrontation extends beyond literally 30 seconds, people begin to run out of energy since they are not used to physical combat, and most lack physical conditioning.

The faster we get done, the better the outcome.

Fighting by its very nature is unsafe. We want to be able to get the bad guy controlled right away. Again, the sooner the better is the safest possible resolution.

Another important concept is element of surprise. When the assault happens, there is an assumption by the bad guy that since he is bigger and stronger, the woman really has no chance.

That assumption is based on the idea that any resistance will be straight forward, muscle against muscle, head on.

When we use a completely different venue of defense, it creates a surprise element for the bad guy.

He now has to adjust his action to the response that is unfamiliar to him.

We are essentially turning the tables on him.

Since it all happens very quickly, there is no time for that.

He cannot process the new information fast enough.

The end result is - we win, he loses.

There is pretty extensive research in the basic human response to suddenly changing, unexpected events.

In police applications, it is called **action versus reaction.**

Let me explain how it works by using a typical scenario.

Let's say a Police Officer enters a room and there is a person standing there with a gun in his hand. The gun is pointed down towards the ground. The officer then will pull out his or hers own firearm and point it at the subject (police name for the bad guy). The officer will tell them to **put the gun down.**

Sometimes the subject will comply and that situation will then be resolved.
Unfortunately, sometimes the subject will quickly raise

the gun and shoot the officer before he or she can fire their weapon.

How can that be?

What happens is that when the subject starts to raise his gun, it takes time for the officer's brain to process that information and then respond. This creates a delay.

Therefore, action is faster than reaction.

When a regular person, not a police officer, is confronted with extraordinary circumstances and an immediate threat, they often freeze.

That is a perfectly normal response of someone without prior training, at a loss as to what to do.

When we look at tragic events like Columbine, Virginia Tech, or recently at Sandy Hook Elementary School, in Newtown, Connecticut, there are a very high number of innocent people getting killed.
Why is that? The answer is that unfortunately, these victims were clearly not prepared to deal with that kind of threat.

There was no effective training in place prior to address it and therefore no practical way to defend them.

The only way to change that and create an ability to quickly and effectively mount a defense, is through training.
Not just physical training. A lot of it has to do with the

mental attitude.

Often times people have an unrealistic view of their environment. They believe that we live in some kind of utopian version of Disney World, where the birds are always singing something like **we are the world.**

This belief leaves many vulnerable. **Vulnerable** to assault since they don't even consider the possibility that something like that can happen to them.

When it does happen, they freeze, which makes them unable to respond and they get hurt or killed. It some instances, this **can** be prevented. It all starts with a realistic assessment of the outside world.

It is true that most people are nice and would not try to hurt anybody.

It is also true that there are some people who actually do want to hurt you. Not a large percentage but they **are** out there.

It is difficult to relate to that kind of thinking. We just need to acknowledge that it does exist.

We have people who are mentally ill within our society.

Some people are on drugs.

Some people are just evil.

This is actually irrelevant.
In other words, we do not care why the bad guy is

assaulting you. We just want to make sure you do not get hurt.

We need to have an effective system to counter the threat. That does not mean that we have to be paranoid. Not at all.

I call this mental preparation **a theory of positive surprise.** It implies that we should look at the world around us with an understanding things can go wrong.

I recommend playing various scenarios out in your mind from time to time, and having a plan of what you are going to do when any situation turns dangerous.

If you notice, I said when, not if. It means

I really do expect something can go wrong. Most of the time it won't happen and I will be positively surprised. Hence, the **theory of positive surprise.**

In direct contrast, when something happens, and you have to defend yourself, you need to be ready.

It is the bad guy, who gets a surprise now. It puts the advantage in your favor.

Of course there is a physical component to this. This is where the predator concepts come into play.

Remember, you are the predator. The bad guy is just a big zebra, so to speak.

We have to immediately put him down and get the

confrontation over with.

The technical part of it is actually pretty simple. People learn better by actually going through hands on training that depicts real life scenarios, as opposed to some hypothetical versions of what might happen.

Of course it is important to do it safely.

When I do the training, I emphasize the idea that everything is originally done at a very slow speed.

One reason for this is for the student to clearly see and comprehend what exactly is happening.

Another reason for the slow motion is to prevent injuries.

Unfortunately, traditional self-defense training often results in injuries.

That should not be happening.

When a person gets hurt in training, the only thing he or she learns is to hate training.

That is understandable.

Injury prevention is a critical part of training.

It is actually easier to do some of the practical self-defense applications faster.

As a result, once a person learns to go through the scenario slowly, it is no problem to speed it up for real use.

Furthermore, training has to be customized for different people with varying levels of fitness.

What is perfectly fine for one person, may cause injury to another.

One of the problems with traditional training is that there are people doing the same exercise all at the same time.

That is a recipe for repeated injury.

It is impossible for the instructor to effectively monitor everybody all at once.

People get hurt, and they may be doing the technique incorrectly.

The instructor cannot watch all the students all the time.

Again, there is no way to control that.

In my training, there are only two people doing the technique at one time. That way it is easy to monitor, correct mistakes, and it helps the next pair, since they get to watch the exercise prior to actually doing it. **There is no rush.**

I also believe that when it comes to practical applications, there is no need for numerous techniques.

Less is definitely more.

People cannot remember a lot of information when stressed; they just need some simple, basic applications that work.

That is not to say that we do not need options because we do.

It is not unusual at all to use a technique on one person with great results, only to do the same thing on somebody else with no effect whatsoever.

That is normal, since no two people are exactly the same.

We do need a few options to deal with a variety of bad guys.
Let me illustrate this concept by using an incident that most people remember.

I am referring to the Rodney King video from California.

Police officers there were trying to control the subject (Rodney King). They had to get him handcuffed, searched and put in the police car. That is all they were supposed to accomplish.

The techniques they used, like beating him with a PR-24 (it is just a stick with another handle) were ineffective. Since they had no options, no other techniques to use, they got frustrated and just resorted to kicking, punching, etc.

The blame was placed on these officers.

My take, is that training or lack of, is at fault there.

They should have had other options to deal with the situation. It is natural to use some technique, and have it fail. We just need to continue to the next option until we get the one that works. Sort of like using tools in your toolbox.

Unfortunately, **there is no silver bullet.** There is no perfect technique or guarantee that whatever technique we use will work. The only thing we know for sure, that something will most likely go wrong.

We do not know what, or when, or how.

The mindset has to be there to keep going with different applications until we get the one that works.

This is why we need options, whether in law enforcement or civilian use.

In this particular case, the whole idea of hitting the subject with a stick is based on the concept of pain compliance. That assumes that when the subject feels the pain, he will become cooperative.

Sometimes it does work like that, sometimes it doesn't.

People, under the influence of drugs, alcohol, mentally ill and extremely agitated subjects are often times way beyond pain compliance.

There has to be a different, none pain based solution to get these people under control.

In Rodney King's case, there wasn't.

My students on the police side deal with situations like that all the time. They are common.

They are able to resolve these problems quickly, without people getting hurt, because they have the options and tools (techniques) necessary to address these types of problems.

The ability to deal with the ever changing threat environment is an essential life skill.

It is impossible to predict with any degree of certainty exactly how the confrontation will unfold. It is also unreasonable and simplistic to believe that all people will respond to a particular application in the same fashion.

That is just not the case.

Self Defense for Children.

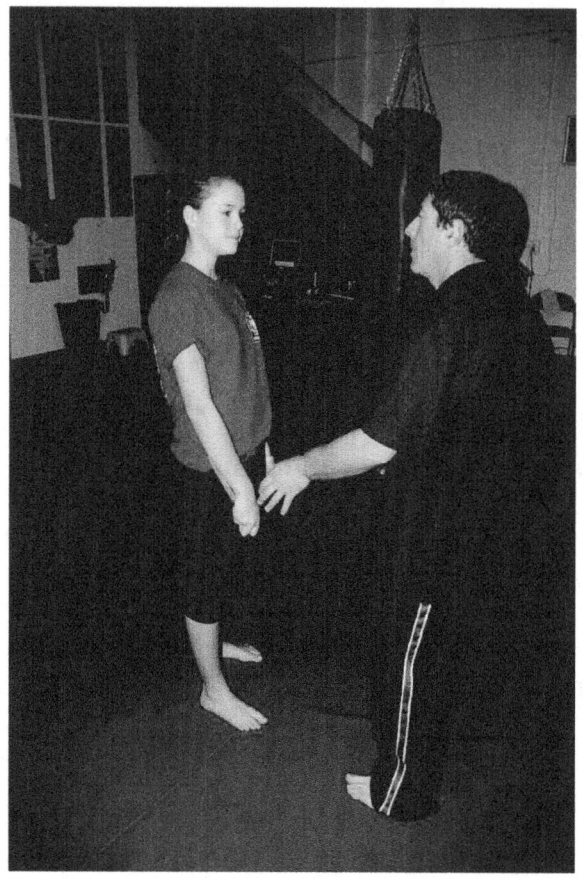

Children really need to be able to defend themselves since they are vulnerable just because they are physically smaller.

On the other hand children learn quickly.

Understanding self-defense for children is an

essential life skill.

Children also confront bullying.

Again, being able to defend themselves gives them confidence.

This in turn deters bullies, when there is no other choice but to stand up.

Would your child know what to do in a situation like Columbine or Virginia Tech, or Sandy Hook?

One reason there were so many casualties when these terrible events took place is that there was no training, and no understanding about dealing with these situations.

Since these acts of violence are random, we can't predict exactly where and when they will occur.

We do know these incidents continue to happen, and it is imperative that children learn what to do when it does happen.

The good news is that children do very well with self-defense.

Here is an example.

I was doing a program for a large sheriff's department in Michigan.

After my training program was concluded, one of the deputies approached me and asked if I could teach his three daughters how to defend themselves.

I was happy to do it.

His youngest daughter was 5 years old. She did great.

Of course when we are talking about teaching children, the simplicity that I advocate for everybody, is even more critical.

They should be able to understand how to defend themselves right away, without going through complicated steps. Their attention span is shorter than an adult's.

They don't want to listen to a long-winded presentation.

Not that anybody should be subjected to that anyway.

Also, children are usually in a lot better physical shape than an average adult. This means that they move faster, and once they break initial contact with the bad guy, they can get away pretty quickly.

Another general point is that children have to learn not to treat everybody they come in contact with as good people.

They have to be told the truth, which means that some people are not good and they have to get away from them.

Again, being mentally prepared makes a difference.

Another point, is that not all children of a certain age have the same maturity level.

I often get a question about the age that a child has to reach when he or she can start learning self-defense. The answer is **it depends.**

Some kids at 10 years old have more maturity that a 15 year old. Some don't.

It is an individual decision based on the individual child.

Overall the benefits of teaching children self-defense are numerous. On a basic level it can literary save their life.

I would say that is definitely worthwhile.

Self Defense Differences.

Men often times develop an overly optimistic and unrealistic opinion of their abilities.
They think that if they have a lot of strength and big muscles, they can overpower anybody.

Sometimes it works like that. **Often** times it does not.

Confrontations are not about muscle. It is the predator versus prey relationship that matters.

Same concepts we discussed before apply here as well.

Remember **eyes in front - born to hunt, eyes on the side - born to hide. You are a predator In a confrontation this is how you must act.**

It is as if the switch went off in your head.

When the situation calls for it, you want to close the distance, grab the bad guy by the head and put him on the ground. And you want to do that right away.

Remember the concept of quick closure.

Again, the longer it takes to get the bad guy under control, the more likely that something will go wrong and you will get hurt.

There were quite a few cases where a police officer would get hurt trying to physically control the subject who was intoxicated, on drugs or mentally unstable by just using force.

Mentally ill people regardless of their physical appearance, can have extraordinary strength.

You don't want to try to overpower them.

It doesn't work.

Again it is not about how big you are or how big the bad guy is. It is all about **tactics.**

Men also have a hard time understanding that they should not to punch the bad guy. I believe the reason for that is primarily cultural. It comes from watching movies and television.

In other words, be a man, put up your dukes, and punch the bad guy in the head.

As I explained earlier, they forgot to mention that this is the recipe for a broken hand.

This is a bad idea.

Unfortunately, most men learn not to punch by actually breaking their hand.

I usually say in my classes that you can either listen to me, which is a lot less painful, or you can break your hand, and then you will know that it was not a good idea.

Let me give you an example. I was once doing a training program for a Law Enforcement agency.

After my class was over, one of the officers came over to speak with me.

He said "I sure wish I met you earlier." He proceeded to tell me that a while back, he pulled over a guy driving a motorcycle.

The guy was wearing a helmet.

One thing led to another and the officer wound up in a confrontation with that guy.

He automatically punched the bad guy in the head (helmet in that case) and broke his hand in four places.

He said he has indeed learned from that experience.

He also pointed out that he never punched anybody again.

I told him that it was really not his fault.

Nobody told him not to punch before. I hear that kind of story often.

On the other hand, men have an easier time than women with the predator concept.

It helps in understanding the overall scope of the confrontation.

Here is another concept: **Forward movement as opposed to backing up.**

Predator moves forward. Prey animals back up.

A typical traditional approach is to step back before confrontation.

There are several problems with that.

First of all moving backwards sends the wrong psychological message to the bad guy. It says "I am afraid, that's why I am backing up."

By the way, some people recommend screaming as a way of getting other people's attention. The assumption there is that people will hear the screaming and come to help you.

Maybe. Maybe not.

I would not count on that.

There have been cases where somebody was assaulted right in front a whole bunch of people who never helped them.

Nowadays people are afraid to help, because they can get sued.

This has already happened.

Another point about screaming shows studies done to establish that people scream because they are afraid.

So that doesn't convey the right message to the bad guy either.

Anyway, back to stepping or moving backwards.

Moving backwards is un-natural.

Think about it.

How often in the course of you everyday life do you actually move backwards while facing forward?

Not really.

The bad guy moving forward will be able to catch up with you pretty easily, since forward motion is natural, and therefore a lot faster.

Also, you cannot see what is behind you.

You do not have your best balance moving backwards.

On the other hand, when you move forward, it makes the bad guy back up.
All the advantage goes to you.

Now he is the one losing his balance, he does not see what is behind him, etc.

Here is something else to consider...

There are some circumstances where we simply cannot go back at all like when we are in a congested space, so there is no room.

Another is when the confrontation goes to the ground.

If you are on your back on the ground, clearly you can't back up. So we are going to go forward through the target. No backing up.

Firearms Applications.

There are a lot of misconceptions associated with firearm use for self-defense.

Again, the TV portrayal is not realistic and is misleading.

When watching some kind of action movie, we often see the person getting shot.

Next, that person is in the air flying backwards, then they go right through the big window, and then there is a fall from a tall building. Wow!

Seems pretty effective.

If you see that representation over and over, you begin to believe that this is how it is going to happen.

Actually this is not true.

That was a "Made for Hollywood" movie.

It does not work like that in real life at all.

What really happens is very different.

There is a lot of data based on real situations. It shows often times the bad guy will get shot repeatedly and still continue to function and do the wrong thing.

Military personnel, police officers and just regular people have been hurt and even killed by bad guys who were shot and should have died, but didn't.

There are several reasons for this.

One is that the location of bullet impact in a human body makes a difference.

This is called **"shot placement"**.

If the bullet hits a non-vital area, the bad guy will continue to function sometimes without any indication that he has been shot or injured at all.

Another myth is that when a person gets shot, they will automatically fall down and die.

It can happen.

Usually it doesn't.

Just because somebody gets shot, does not mean that they are dead. It also does not mean that all their function is lost.

There are a lot of people who are alive today after they have been shot. Some of them received serious wounds that could have killed them. Yet they **survived. That is a very important point.**

It means we cannot assume that the threat is stopped just because we shot the bad guy.
The flip side of that coin means that even if we get shot, we most likely can continue to function and defend ourselves.

There are some incredible actual cases of people doing just that.

It is critical to have a positive mental attitude. Here is an example;

There was a female police officer, who was off duty at a time. She approached her car and was carjacked.

The bad guy shot her through the heart with a 357 round.

That is a big bullet.

She returned fire and shot the bad guy.

When the ambulance arrived at the scene, they saw the location of the wound and didn't think there was anything they could do for her. But they did what they could, since that is what they are trained to do, and drove her to the hospital.

Once she arrived at the hospital, again her chances did not look good.

She was taken in for emergency surgery and amazingly, she is alive and functioning today.

There are numerous examples of similar incidents.

It is definitely mind over matter.

Here is another example that really drives the point home.

My friend, Duane shared this with me. Duane teaches at a Criminal Justice College in Minnesota. I actually met him at the ILEETA (International Law Enforcement Educators and Trainers Association) Conference in Chicago, Illinois where he was teaching a course on OODA LOOP (Observation, Orientation, Decision and Action).
I will address the OODA LOOP later.

Anyway, Duane gave a compelling example that actually happened to his student, a police officer in Minnesota. One day he was responding to a call where he had to enter a house. Almost immediately the bad guy fired his weapon at him. The officer got hit and fell down.

Somebody else could have quit and died. Not this officer. He got up and returned fire and stayed in the fight. The officer literally recalls hearing Duane's voice in his head, saying "he has to keep going".
The officer continued to engage and shoot at the bad guy. He was able to stop the threat. He also survived his injuries.

Duane recalls getting a call from his fellow officer crediting him with saving his life.

That is a clear example of the critical importance of positive mental attitude. It is also an example where good, relevant training can save your life.

Let me explain the OODA Loop.

Colonel John Boyd was a fighter pilot and he is credited with creating the OODA Loop.

OODA stands for Observation, Orientation, Decision and Action.

United States fighter pilots and other branches of the military now use these concepts.

John Boyd explains how we go through that process under stress.

According to John, training shortens the OODA Loop and allows you to respond to the threat faster.

He applied this concept to training fighter pilots with exceptional results.

We apply the same concept to any kind of critical response under stressful conditions.

We want to get inside the OODA Loop of the bad guy so that he is unable to function because there is no time for him to complete his OODA Loop, and by the time he gets to the Action part of the Loop, we have already won the confrontation.

This is just the gist of it.

You can Google OODA Loop or John Boyd for more detailed explanation. Suffice to say it is an important concept and it does work.

Back to people's responses to being shot...

Unfortunately, sometimes people have died after receiving survivable wounds, because they believed what they saw on TV - you get shot - you die. This is an example where the wrong kind of thinking can kill you.

By the way, the state of medical care makes a huge difference as well.

Years ago, when a soldier was wounded in battle, he was very likely to die. Maybe not even from the wound, but the infection. Medical science has truly come a very long way since then.

Nowadays people receive wounds that would have killed them for sure in the past and they survive. It matters how fast they get to the hospital. The faster the better.

Again, chances of survival even with serious wounds are a lot better now.

The size of the bullet makes a difference as well. Obviously, a bigger and heavier bullet has more energy and more stopping power than a smaller, lighter one. It is important to understand though, that using a bigger bullet is not an excuse for poor shot placement.

Generally speaking, when it comes to bullets having stopping power, bigger is better.

The shape of the bullet is another factor. Without getting too technical, I will just say that a military style, full metal jacket bullet has very different characteristics from a typical hollow point round.

Not all bullets are created equal. Not at all. Not all weapons are created equal as well.

Some people like firearms. Some don't.

Without regard to one's preferences, or should I say likes and dislikes, it is important becoming familiar with different types of firearms. You never know when that understanding can save your life.

You want to be able to instantly recognize the type of weapon. You may have to use it to save your life. Ignorance can be deadly. There are handguns, shotguns and rifles just to name the basic types you are likely to encounter out there. These weapons are distinct and have different characteristics.

In other words, weapons are not all the same, and knowing the differences is quite valuable.

Handguns have a short barrel and can be easily concealed. That makes them practical for a person to carry when out in public.
When people get a CCW (carrying concealed weapon) or CPL (concealed pistol license) they usually carry some kind of handgun.

These are basically a defensive type of weapon and they are designed for close distances. That is not to say you can't use a handgun to shoot at a longer range. You can. It is just not designed for that application. Usually a short barrel means close distance, longer barrel - longer distance.

There are two types, revolvers and semi-automatics. Revolvers have a cylinder that rotates when the weapon is fired and generally holds 6 rounds. Some people like them and still use them.

Originally most handguns were revolvers. Semi-automatics can carry more rounds depending on the caliber. They came into their own later.

Again, the advantage of the handgun is its fairly small size, which makes it easy to conceal.
More and more people prefer semi-automatic weapons, since they are easy to operate and reload and generally have less recoil, depending on the design and caliber.

The semi-automatic weapon will fire a round every time the trigger is pressed until all the rounds are fired. Then the slide of the weapon will lock to the rear and it will need a new magazine with fresh ammo to resume firing.

Shotguns are a lot more powerful than the handguns. They are substantially longer and heavier. The effective range of a shotgun, depending on the type of load, is longer than the handgun, although its best use is still fairly close.

The shotgun is an ideal weapon to defend yourself at home with since the distances within the house are fairly short.

Shotguns are versatile weapons that can shoot a variety of different loads.

Shotguns can be manually operated, like a pump shotgun, or semi-automatic.

One characteristic of a shotgun is that it has substantial recoil. Some people are comfortable with it. Women are often times bothered by heavy recoil.

That brings us to rifles. They are manually operated rifles, like a bolt action, lever action, or a pump. There are also semi-automatic rifles. Semiautomatic rifles, depending on the caliber, have a lot less recoil in comparison with a shotgun.

A compact version of a rifle can also be used effectively for home defense. You don't want a long weapon in the close quarters, because it is difficult to maneuver with it.

Rifles have a long effective range. They can be fired accurately over long distances.

Handguns, shotguns and rifles look very different from each other. Once you are familiar with them, you can tell what kind of weapon it is instantly.

Firearms Training.

Traditional firearms training was done as target practice. The target was standing still. The shooter didn't move. People were told to watch their front sight, point the weapon at the center of the target's chest and slowly squeeze the trigger.

That system works for target practice. On the other hand, that is not what typically happens in real life. The bad guy normally does not stand still. He is moving. You don't want to stand still either, because it makes you an easy target for the bad guy.

Most confrontations happen at a very close range, just several feet apart. At that distance people will not look at their front sight, but instead focus on the bad guy. Also, shooting center mass, or at the center of the chest often times does not stop the bad guy.

There are numerous **real life** cases when the bad guy gets shot center mass and instead of stopping, continues to move and shoot. Therefore, it is critical to have training that deals with the real life applications as opposed to target practice.

People under stressful conditions will do what they are trained to do. Let me use an actual shooting incident to illustrate this point.

It happened in North Hollywood, California about 10 years ago. Two heavily armed subjects took over a bank and started to shoot when police showed up. They were wearing body armor on the outside of their clothing. It was clearly visible. The police shot them numerous times with the regular pistol ammunition. It had no effect at all because of the body armor and because they were shooting center mass.

Eventually, after a lot of people got hurt, the SWAT team was able to bring the bad guys down. It was a miracle that nobody got killed.

There are several issues stemming from that shooting incident. Since the bad guy's body armor was clearly visible, why did the officers continue to shoot them center mass?

When people are exposed to extremely stressful circumstances, they respond automatically. They just do what they trained to do. It is impossible for them to figure things out and change on the spot. There is no time for that. This is why I am a believer in relevant training. In other words, training has to resemble real life circumstances, not sterilized make belief conditions at the range.

Lt. Col. David Grossman in his book "On Killing" gives another good example of people blindly doing what they were trained to do in a war environment.

He speaks about soldiers during World War I, who trained to shoot at a bullseye type of target.

Bullseye targets look like a solid black circle on a square white background. When these soldiers deployed into the theatre of operations, a high percentage of them (I believe around 80%) did not engage the enemy. This means they did not shoot at the enemy soldiers. That sounds amazing, yet it actually makes sense. The enemy soldiers did not look like a bullseye they shot at in practice. There was a disconnect between training and reality. During the Vietnam war the rate of engagement (how many soldiers actually fired at the enemy) went over 90%.

The reason is because targets were changed to look like enemy soldiers. Problem corrected. **That** is what I mean by relevant training.

Let's address movement. Most people have a difficult time engaging (shooting) moving targets. Again, they usually shoot at a standing target in practice.

I believe that it is unreasonable to ask a person to effectively shoot a moving target in real life, when they never did it in training.

A good example of engaging moving targets is skeet shooting. Skeet shooting started out as a system to help bird hunters hit birds in flight.

By the way, we use shotguns with light loads for that training exercise. Obviously, we can't ask the bird to stand still in the air, so that we can line up our sights and slowly squeeze the trigger. I wish we could. It would be so much easier. It helps to understand the relationship between the shot and the bird, that is flying through the air.

It's just like in a game of football. When the quarterback throws the ball to the receiver who is in motion, he has to throw it ahead of the receiver. That is called **the lead.** That way by the time the ball gets there, the receiver will be there as well.

If the ball is thrown right at the receiver, since he keeps running, it will wind up behind him.

That is the physics of shooting moving targets. The concept again is that the shot and the bird are in motion and will meet at some spot ahead of their current position.

That is a crucial point to understand. It explains why we shoot ahead of the moving target, where it is going to be. By the way, bird hunters understand that right away, since that is how they shoot.

Even more important is to understand why you have to keep moving when somebody is shooting at you.

Since most people have no idea of how to shoot a moving target, they will usually shoot right at it, as if it were standing still. Their shot will go behind you, because there is no denying the laws of physics.

Of course, anything can go wrong. You can still get shot. But, your chances are a lot better when you do the right thing, which is to **keep moving.**

There is a big difference between shooting standing targets and engaging moving ones. One example of relevant purpose training is to teach a person how to move and shoot at the same time. The military calls it: shoot, move and communicate. I agree.

Communicating is a good idea as well.

The next issue is shot placement. As I pointed out, it matters where the bullet impacts the bad guy. Shoot him in the right place, and he will stop. Shoot him in the wrong place, and he will keep going.

What is the right place then? I would say that a shot that will stop a bad guy instantly is placed correctly.

Again, we do not shoot the bad guy, just to shoot him. We want him to stop. Often times the traditional center mass shot or shots does not accomplish that.

Why is that? Well, maybe the bad guy has body armor, as in the example we used before. Even if there is no body armor, often times center mass shot fails to accomplish immediate stop of the bad guy's actions. To understand it we have to look into inner workings of the human body.

The center mass shot will hit vital organs, such as heart and lungs. The problem is that the brain is still functioning.

As long as there is blood with oxygen in the brain, it will continue to operate, and the bad guy can continue to fire his weapon. Eventually, if we stopped the hearty putting a round through it, the blood from the brain will drain down, the blood pressure will go to zero and the bad guy will stop. It does not happen right away though. It may take several seconds or more leaving plenty of time for the bad guy to shoot you.

Remember that most confrontations happen up close and very personal.

The question then becomes can the bad guy be stopped right away at all?

Here the good news. Yes, he can be stopped right away. To do this we have to shoot him through the head.

Yes, we are back to head control. Just like a sniper.

To make this point I recollect pictures I saw on the internet. There was one of those insurgent bombers in Iraq or Afghanistan. He was about to detonate his vest full of explosives and kill innocent people around him. A marine sniper shot him in the head and he dropped right away. He was not able to detonate the explosives because the head shot stopped all his motor functions instantly. That shot saved all those people.

At a close range it is possible for us to do the same thing. What I am saying is the shot we are looking for is a head shot. To stop the bad guy right away, instantly.

Some people will argue that it is difficult to do. Actually it is not. It is easier that shooting center mass. This is a lot more effective. One reason is that the head is our natural focus.

We are already automatically looking there. Remember we are very close to the threat.

There is another important point to be made here. If you picture yourself in front of the bad guy, pointing your weapon at him center mass, he can still see you. This means he can shoot you.

Now if you point your weapon right at his head, his focus automatically shifts to looking at the barrel of your weapon, from looking at you. He does not see you anymore. Of course it all happens quickly. But now you can shoot the bad guy, and he has no visual on you and therefore can't shoot you.

Again, shot placement is critical.

Now let's talk about looking at sights on your weapon. Naturally your instinct is to look at the bad guy. Just like when you throw the ball. You are focused at the glove, not looking at your finger. Looking at the finger is like looking at your sights. The natural way, looking at the glove is like looking at the bad guy. So let me put all these concepts together.

When confronted by a bad guy, who is threatening your life, you want to respond effectively. That involves shooting on the move, shooting through the head and looking at your target, rather than your sights. When we are that close to the bad guy, your movement is forward, through the target. No backing up (familiar concept).

These are just some basic ideas. There are training exercises to put all that into practice.

By the way, shooting natural way is a lot easier that doing it in the traditional fashion. This is a lot more user friendly.

Unfortunately nowadays people get themselves through the CCW class where they learn target shooting the stationary way, and then they believe that they know what they are doing.

Interestingly, the bad guy has several advantages relative to the police officer or regular citizen. The bad guy has no hesitation. He genuinely does not care that he is killing you. He does not care if his bullets miss you and hit other innocent people.

It is difficult for a normal person to comprehend that attitude. We are not like that. It is critical to understand that though. By the time we get into life threatening situation, we just need to stop the threat. That is all.

Also, the bad guy has often times no traditional training. Nobody told him to stand still, breath in, breath out and slowly press the trigger. He just points his weapon and shoots. No thinking involved. Everything happens very fast.

One more thing... Video games. Think of them as shooting simulators.

Often times the bad guys play these video games. This actually prepares them for the real thing.

In the video games you have to shoot fast and you get extra points for shooting in the head.

So the bad guy is not an easy target. But understanding how it really works makes a huge difference.

Remember again that the winning attitude is extremely important.

One more thing... **It is important to notice that this whole training concept is focused on the head control. Control the head - control the bad guy.**

Here is a good visual example of head control.

When you watch the rodeo, there is an event there called steer wrestling.

What happens is that a steer runs forward and the cowboy chases after him on horseback. When he catches up with the steer, the cowboy jumps from his horse and grabs the steer by the head. Then he twists the head putting his weight on it, just like a predator would (remember the lioness), and the steer goes down.

The whole process from start to finish only takes a few seconds. Actually the guy with the fastest time wins the event. I am sure most people have seen it either in person or on TV.

Let's analyze this example. The steer is huge. Definitely much bigger and stronger than any bad guy. Yet we can put him down using the head control principle.

That is exactly how it works in real life, except it is a lot easier, since the bad guy has never seen it before and has no idea as to what is happening.

Whether we just grab the bad guy by the head and put him down, because the threat level was pretty low, or we have to shoot him through the head, because the situation was life threatening, one thing remains the same; That is that head is like your computer's hard drive or main breaker in your house, or, as the military puts it, command and control, we have to control it. You control the head, you control the whole subject (bad guy).

You can think that a head shot, when the situation calls for it (life threatening circumstances), is the ultimate form of head control.

Ground Applications.

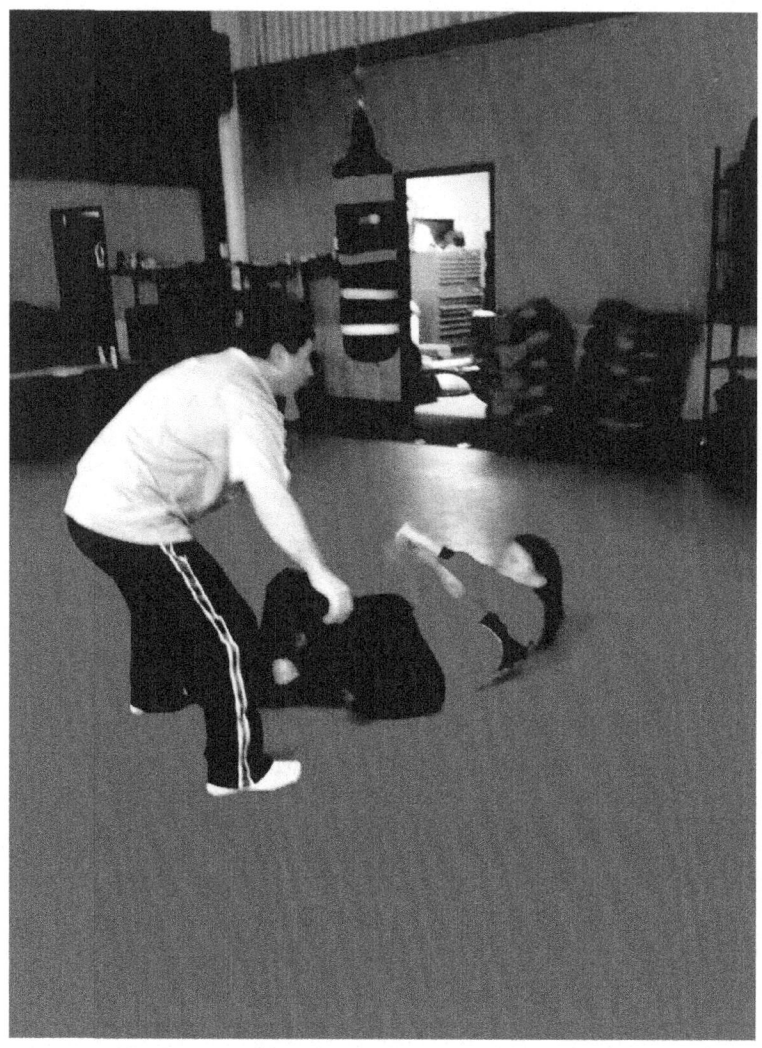

Ground self defense got a bad name for **NO** good reason. Again, I think it is cultural. You would hear statements like: if you are down, you are out, or let's see who is left standing. The implication is that being on the ground is bad, you are in a bad position.

That is not true at all. You may be down, but you are not out.

Ground is actually a pretty good place. You recall my example with the lioness. She takes the zebra to the ground. Apparently it is not a bad place for her. People are justifiably concerned because they have no idea as to what they are going to do when they wind up on the ground.

Good news... There are simple practical applications dealing with ground situations.

As an example, we can look at vascular neck restraint. That's a mouthful.

Let me explain. The word vascular is just a medical term meaning blood flow.

Neck means neck. Pretty self-explanatory.

Restraint is the word I like.

First of all, having restraint is a good idea. You don't want to get all excited and loose your cool. Bad things can happen as a result.

In this particular case, vascular neck restraint simply means the restriction of the blood (remember vascular) flow to the head.

Again, it's all about head control. There is an airway

located right in the middle of the neck.

We are not going to do anything with it.

On both sides of the airway there is a carotid artery. That artery supplies blood with oxygen to the brain. Vascular neck restraint stops the blood flow through the carotid artery, interrupting the blood supply to the brain.

This results in the bad guy passing out and don't confuse it with a "choke hold".

It doesn't take long. When done correctly, within about 3 seconds the bad guy will go from zero to pass out, unlike a choke hold restricting air intake to the lungs.

It is an excellent technique. It is simple, easy to learn and works great and is very effective.

The typical application is on the ground. It is like flipping the switch. You can take a real bad guy, who may be high on drugs or mentally ill, or both, and just turn him off without injury.

In a choke hold, you can easily damage someone's airway or wind pipe which I do not recommend. There are many documented uses of vascular neck restraint.

So, as you can see, this is just one example of things we can do on the ground.

By the way, vascular neck restraint can be applied in just about any position relative to the bad guy.

Again, this is a great technique.

Edged Weapons.

My program on edged weapons became especially popular after the terrible events of September 11th, 2001. The terrorists brought down planes using box cutters, basically small knives. Is it possible to defend against a knife or a box cutter, or any kind of edged weapon. Yes, it is. It helps to understand how to deal with that threat.

People have used sharp objects since the stone age. All weapons used to be some form of an edged weapon. They were, and still are very effective. Especially at close range since that is where most confrontations take place. It makes these weapons very much relevant in the overall picture of self defense applications. Just about anything with a sharp edge will cause damage. Again, the television and movie version of knife confrontation is not what really happens.

Just about any action movie has a scene where the bad guy holds the knife and is coming down with it. The person defending himself grabs the hand with the knife with both hands and it becomes a contest of strength, with the knife's blade getting closer or father from the good guy. It looks dramatic, but it is **not** realistic.

This is what can happen in real life. All the bad guy has to do is tilt the blade down and cut the hand holding his arm. The natural instinct is then to grab the arm that is cut, which breaks the hold and leaves the good guy wide open. It very easy to do and this is just one option.

Here is another point. Usually the TV version shows the bad guy stabbing with the knife. Stabbing is not that effective. The knife blade can get stuck.

Sometimes the bad guy can actually cut his hand with his own knife. That happens when the knife hits a hard target, like the sternum. The knife stops and the hand can slide down on the blade, which will cut it.

Cutting is a lot more effective and easier to do. Again, most confrontations happen very much up close and personal. That leaves them open to all kinds of edged weapons. It is a good idea to have an edged weapon of your own and to know what to do with it. There is no need for a big knife. It is hard to conceal and difficult to maneuver.

All we need is a small knife that is very sharp. I prefer the design that has a clip. It will then clip to the pant pocket and can be easily deployed using one hand.

Some have a reversible clip that can be moved from one side of the knife to the other. That enables a person to use their left hand or right hand with the same knife design.

The two sides of edged weapons, have to do with understanding how to defend against them and how to use one for self-defense.

Another point relating to edged weapons is that they are light, small, easy to conceal and carry. Also, you do not need a permit to carry them, except that the size of the blade is usually restricted. We don't need a big blade anyway.

Some people like to carry a handgun. Some people carry a knife. I think we should carry both, depending on the circumstances.

Sometimes you can just carry a knife, because of the clothing you wear. I like to have options. Anything can go wrong with any piece of equipment.

We have to be prepared to continue to function even when equipment fails.

If you were using a firearm and run out of ammunition, or it jammed, you can just transition to the knife and keep defending yourself. With the knife, you not are going to run out of ammo (ammunition).

Sometimes we use what are called **weapons of opportunity.** These are tools that are not designed to be used as a weapon but can function in that capacity.

For example, in prison inmates often times make their own deadly edged weapons made out of whatever materials they can find. They use screwdrivers, needles, sharpened spoons, tooth brushes etc. They call these weapons shanks.

There was a case where a mentally ill man broke a window. Then he picked up a piece of glass and used that as an edged weapon.

The type of damage inflicted by the edged weapon is different from that of a bullet impact. While bullet creates a wound channel in a body and a hydraulic shock, the cutting action of the knife creates bleeding. If an artery is cut (like carotid or femoral), a person can quickly die from loss of blood (bleed out).

The Importance of Vision.

Human beings have five senses. By far the most important is the sense of sight.

Over 90% of our perception of outside world is visual. Over 30% of our brain is dedicated to dealing with visual information. This information and understanding has profound implications in reference to self-defense. We have to have a clear view of the bad guy in order to effectively deal with the threat. Ideally, we don't want the bad guy to have any visual of us.

For example, our best position is behind the bad guy's back, so that he can't see us. In my example earlier, when the lioness goes after the zebra, she closes the distance to get within range using any available cover in order to stay out of sight of the zebra. The bad guy can be a mentally ill or high on drugs. Still, If he can't see you, he can't hurt you, without regard to anything else.

That's why the very first thing we have to do in a confrontation is to disengage his vision.

Just as an example, let's say the bad guy tried to grab you. Traditionally people were taught to beat on his arms to break the hold. I am not a fan of that.

If the bad guy is bigger and stronger than you, you will not be able to do it. Also, it is hard to do. One of the basic principles I apply is **if it is hard to do, I don't do it.** I like things that are easy to do. There no reason to make it difficult.

The confrontation to me is not about strength. So rather than struggle trying to break the hold, you can just use an open handed stun. It is basically a slap to the bad guy's head.

Let me explain how that works.

The brain inside the head is not bolted to the sides. It actually floats in cerebral (brain) fluid. When the head is hit with the open hand (not a punch, you don't want to break your hand, remember), a waive goes through the head. The bad guy literally sees the light (or stars). He often will collapse right there.

By the way, on the police side of my business we use that particular application every day with great results. Once the bad guy drops, it's time to leave.

Don't stand there and admire your work. Again, the open handed stun to the face (away from the mouth) makes the bad guy see the light. Literally. He **can't** see you.

It is all about visual. You should have a clear view of the bad guy.

Situational awareness.

Situational awareness means seeing and responding to your surroundings.

Paying attention. Often times people are going about their business without any regard to what is going on around them. It is like they are oblivious to everything (wearing headphones, listening to music, texting and walking, etc.) Their focus is inwards. That is, the kind of attitude that gets them hurt. We have to acknowledge that the outside world can turn hostile and dangerous in a hurry. There is a certain baseline, normal functioning that usually takes place around us.

Sometimes there is a deviation from that baseline routine. Something is different. It doesn't look right. Often times you have a feeling that something is wrong. They call it **intuition.** Do **NOT** ignore it.

By the way women are a lot better at it than men.

Anyway, when you get that feeling, it's time to leave. Your intuition is usually right. You don't want to stay and find out that you were right, and now you have to physically defend yourself. It is always **BEST** to avoid confrontation. Remember that.

Another important concept is minimizing exposure. That means you have to assess you daily activity from the stand point of threat management.

As an example, let's say you decided to go on vacation. Some place nice and warm. You have options.

You could go to Mexico, Florida or Hawaii. From the stand point of minimizing exposure, I would go to either Florida or Hawaii. It is a **lot** safer. That doesn't mean you can't go to Mexico. You just have to realize that there are a lot of security problems there.

If something goes wrong don't expect the U.S. government to come get you.

Conclusion.

As I said in the beginning, my mission is to help people. To empower them with knowledge and understanding, so they will be able to defend themselves.

Because of my extensive work with Law Enforcement, I have a unique perspective on self-defense, since the concepts and techniques I teach are used every day in real life situations with excellent results. Therefore my knowledge is not hypothetical, but practical.

It is not my opinion as to whether these concepts will work in real life, but the experience of actually using them and seeing them work.

This book covers basic concepts of self defense for women, children, men, and Law Enforcement. It addresses dealing with firearms, firearm training, edged weapons, ground applications, importance of vision and situational awareness. It deals with basic self-defense concepts, such as being a predator, not prey, moving forward through the target, having a positive mental attitude, quick closure and winning the confrontation.

I want to thank you for taking the time to read my book. I know that these ideas will work for you, as they have for countless others faced with dangerous situations. You can always contact me with any questions.

My website is: www.shaykhettraining.com. Contact information is provided there.

Made in the USA
Monee, IL
16 November 2022